You Were That White Bird

You Were That White Bird

SHELLEY GIRDNER

Bauhan Publishing
Peterborough New Hampshire
2016

Library of Congress Cataloging-in-Publication Data
Names: Girdner, Shelley, author.Title: You were that white bird : poems /
Shelley Girdner.
Description: Peterborough, NH : Bauhan Publishing, 2016.
Identifiers: LCCN 2015050639 | ISBN 9780872332201 (pbk. : alk. paper)
Classification: LCC PS3607.I4695 A6 2016 | DDC 811/.6--dc23
LC record available at http://lccn.loc.gov/2015050639

Book design by Kirsty Anderson.
Typeset in Bembo Book Pro with titles in Michael Harvey's "Ellington."
Cover design by Henry James.
Cover photo from ©SwedePix.
Photo of the author by David Ramsay.
Manufactured by Kase Printing.

BAUHAN
PUBLISHING LLC
PO BOX 117 PETERBOROUGH NEW HAMPSHIRE 03458
603-567-4430
WWW.BAUHANPUBLISHING.COM

Manufactured in the United States of America.

For my white birds: Henry, Josiah, and Steve.

Contents

You were that white bird

Before there were birds

We said, god give us birds, by having no words
for love or hope, and then there they were—

nimble and blurred bright enough
we thought we'd lost our sight

only to recover it in found nests,
feathers left, the marvel of the early skeletons,

the way they showed even bone
could be different from bone.

The eggs, too: out slid the yellow eye
of where they flew, as if they'd caught suns

again and again in their bodies.
Cracking one open was the first we knew:

there were worlds we could make
other than shelter, other than fire.

The way desire works

Green stamps

Everything was sad in the green stamp store,
yet how could that be when so much joy went into getting there?

The cheery spools beside registers in grocery stores,
spitting out ribbons of stamps by the foot, by the yard.

Irrepressible were the evenings spent licking and gluing
stamps to their booklets, the thin pages wavy with spit.

Each new page was a blank grid like a bingo board
you could win from. You kept the stamps in a big plastic bag:

optimism was touching it, knowing it contained
all you wanted, the way a cloud holds rain.

But something is always to be lost in conversion:
the hours poured into those booklets were no different.

What brought you there—the sewing machine, the
handheld radio—long ago sold out or discontinued.

The shelves mostly empty, the clerks suspicious of people
with time and green stamps enough to buy anything big

but bored with the small-ticket items. Yellow umbrellas
from PVC patio sets leaned like felled trees. Stacks of feeding bowls

and hamster wheels were knowing holes. Isn't this the way desire always works?
The end of wanting bringing with it another kind of want:

you traded for the rabbit cage without the rabbit in it.

AD + SG 4 ever

"I love you, Albrecht Dürer!"
I shout in the dark art history class,
when a slide of your self-portrait
is broadcast to wall-sized dimensions.
Your ringleted hair and luxe fur jacket proof,
the professor says, of your egotism.
I look at your soul-deep eyes, large enough
on the screen for me to stand upright inside,
and feel like an embryo the moment
it splits itself in half.

I'm not worried about other women or men
feeling the same way. Albrecht, you and I
made a pact centuries ago.
We are like the portrait of Dorian Gray:
it's the relationship we would have had
that grows older in the attic, while out in the world
there is always a jolt between us; first-touch love,
still shooting sparks, enough to light
a Christmas tree or a small parking lot.

I'll never have to get used to you,
we must have whispered
in that smoke-burnished vestibule
of the 15th century, pressing our bulky rings
into hot wax.

But Albrecht,
our calculations were wrong:
there are only so many times I can stand
to stand in front of your portrait, open
an expensive art book to the dog-eared page.
A rat hit over the head repeatedly
either dies or learns to stop wincing.
I'm lonely, Albrecht.
I want to tear up that contract
or burn it in the basement. I want to watch you rise
in a column of smoke, still dandy in tights,
and then get on with it—
the fights and frustrations of life together,
the way we'd have to negotiate our long hair,
always brushing it from each other's face
in order to kiss, your cold feet
at the bottom of the bed,
trying to warm themselves
on mine.

Archetypal Renderings of the Male-Female Relationship
after Louise Bourgeois

If Rita Hayworth were here, she'd throw
a frothy slip over the top of this changing screen
and wink, her eyelashes like mink stoles,
naughty and luxe.

But it's just me behind the privacy divider
and the walled space is like a confessional,
the veneer on the lone stool worn to a moth shape
from the weight of too much sitting and thinking,
too much rocking back and forth on the problem
of a man in my bed this morning, long
as a necklace unclasped in the sheets.

His thinness gnaws me, collarbones jutting
in a way that feels wrong on a man.
I keep thinking, *If he's ever caught naked
in a rainstorm, they'll fill up like birdbaths.*

Always, it's his hollows that trouble me,
even the vacant peace on his face while he sleeps.
I know he's keeping a cave inside him, complete
with vague drawings on the wall, buffalo
going down and figures dancing around
a fire—a whole host of markings
and none of them mine.

We Used to Call Ourselves Kali

We found a bunch of broken bottles once
and ground them down with our boot heels; glass
embedded in the soles. The scritchscratch of our steps
afterward made us laugh while others cringed.

In each other's company, we were like that, haughty and blue-
skinned from wearing too little in the night air. It was destruction
we dreamed we painted on our nails, black rims that sank
into every man; we kissed and kissed them more,
then slunk through back doors to meet up and laugh again.

Without fear or futures yet, we walked late, drank
too much, and dodged the bill. We said *shut the fuck up*
and could sense repercussions bucking but
bucking far afield. We used to call ourselves Kali,

a feeling between us that isn't there anymore.
As if weighted to sink, we let her drop, our past life
like a bottle plugged and tossed. She disappeared
so convincingly it's as if she never existed
or that she's separate from us, sealed in a jar like djinn.

My matryoshkas

Greedy doll, so greedy you swallowed
four more like you, each with a rosebud mouth,
matching floral blouse, and hair kerchief too.
I take you apart in demitasses,
half cup after half cup girl.

I can't ever decide if you're meant to be
sisters, daughters, or a woman
with her past stacked inside her.
I pause over your smallest one,
curved as a spindle.

Is she the baby about to be imprinted,
taught to be a woman with earrings
and black hair held back from her face
in swoops like the swallow's tail?
Or is she the end of the line,

the last chance to be otherwise?
The least ornate, she's the only thing solid.
Sometimes, she's the soul to me,
the tongue of conscience clicking against
the hollow wants of the world.

Others, she's sadder: when we're born,
we're this way, all encased, and despite
the growth, the paint, the layers put on,
there's still a nub, the bit we push at
but can never make open.

Thrift-store purses

Empty of their tissues, pens, coupons, receipts, tampons, lists,
lipsticks, hair elastics, lint, even the crumbs of some bit of food,
they sag. Cheap leather, if leather at all. Navies and dark greens,
staid colors of '80s women's power suits, remnant of when
the whole world was working toward a gray room.

Nowhere in this display are the clutches, satin-wrapped for evening,
or the white and appliqué bags girls carry at Easter. Those trinkets
of specific moments, of parties tipping on high heels,
never make it here, having been stuffed with newsprint and folded away.
With pleasure to be pulled out later, opened absently and searched
for coins like half-dollars, long out of use.

Hasn't it always been strange to you, the relationship
to mouth, the way the purse is safest when it's shut,
and yet with your own lips gathered you're too aware
of what's bundled on either side, looking to be let out.

The reply

I was just describing myself as at loose ends
when a black bow tie showed up all on its own in the dirt
of the path where I was walking, as if in reply
to a personal ad I'd placed without knowing.
There was nothing but the bow left, part of a fake,
a knot once hot-glued or quick-stitched to a strip of fabric,
made to look legit in a way it can't now, last kiss

of a formal event that must have ended in a goofy striptease
with the necktie popping off like a button
or in retching, a man drunk and leaning,
trying to snatch the black bloom from his throat.

After such abandonment I have no choice but to claim it,
balance it out in my palm as if a bird learning to fly
after long healing.

I bring it home, lay it out with your clothes,
rest it on your pillow. It floats there, attached to a kite
I can't see, an hourglass turned on its side.

Later, I'll wear it in my hair like a black butterfly
bringing its bit of loss and night
wherever I go.

Prequel: Hansel and Gretel's Stepmother

This is her dumb luck: at parties in her single days,
she was always followed by the belle.
And when she is, at last, the one who follows,
she comes behind the dead wife,
a woman never in the room but always looked for.

And how much worse is it to be with children,
the innocence with which they let their father lift them in his arms?
Perhaps she weeps to see them every morning, their voices
like wands producing whatever they think to desire,
though they do not ask for hard things, just a father home at dinnertime,
a yard full of animals, and each other.
What do they know about being locked out of their own lives?

She spends days plucking petals to the tune
"He loves me; he loves me not," the flowers closer to the source
than her own heart, a mean and beating bird
with eyes only for the petals falling, one by one.
They harden in her like pebbles dropped by another hand
and leading to another home without children or windows,
only her and this man, a single key she keeps tied
around her neck on a pale pink string.

Clairvoyance

A scene: my great-grandmother's kitchen,
an old woman and a boy play cards.
Look closer:
she holds one card;
the boy closes his eyes,
fingers at temples.
She is teaching him
clairvoyance—
how to unlock
the secret inside her.
In this case:
seven red diamonds
piping a white field.

Another scene: my kitchen,
my father lays the cards aside.
This kind of knowing
takes two people,
seer and seen.
"Your job," he says
with not a little sadness,
his hand heavy
on my left shoulder,
"is to go transparent
when the time comes."

And I do
with you around.

I turn thick glass,
a snow globe, my heart
the tiny, painted village,
the one light burning there.
You're the watcher and the hand
that shakes me into snow,
this attempt to obscure
even slightly
what I have laid
so bare.

The long picnic

First frost laces their eyelashes shut. They are sprawled on a blanket with a basketful of food even the ants won't touch. His summer broadcloth blanches from red to pink. Her lips chapped purple peel to the same pink, and though they're both awake, each feigns sleep.

With her loose right hand, the left locked in his, she taps a slow code. She asks the grass beneath the blanket to keep growing. She says, *Grow. And grow through me,* wanting the blades to stitch up into her bones, to pin her there.

The field lies back for winter, their blanket, their bodies the only patch of color, while underneath the surface, layers down and sifting, a core of earth melts, solidifies, and melts again.

Two is

symmetry. Two bodies on their sides in the bed like stairsteps, crooked and echoing one another. Two is breath and tide. Is the direction of every path in the world since you can always double back. Two can be a number of balance but isn't a number of peace, as any agreement between two is two separate understandings with no third to observe, to enforce. Push-pull, it's true, two can equal but can't cancel out. That is the defiance of two. Children at this age are infamously stubborn. When you have a test and only two questions, you sweat. Dinner for two is a date. There's a kind of spotlight we expect to happen with just one, but really, it happens with two. Mostly two is temporary. On the way to becoming more or less. Even that moment with the two on the bed—one is already rolling away.

The sorry apart mirror

It was when you were gone I looked in the mirror and saw our room in reverse, the windows on the wrong side and my hair parted backward. The days were like that, inversions. Close to true but folded on a meridian I couldn't see. What was the divide? I asked, my teeth like the backsides of trees, of scenes that had pivoted away. The mirror knew itself continually. I found I could look a little deeper into it each time but never see back to that night with you on the bed. I did begin noticing lines, a study of them. Horizontal, vertical, a map was forming. I found squares and rectangles where I expected, drawer faces, but also in the negative space (that's a term for where I was!)—symmetrical emptiness surrounded by furniture. I counted the blinds, the individual louvers, the edges that go into making just one baseboard separate from the wall behind it. The room was all kinds of ledges I was jumping from without you in it.

The poem

Like an animal you thought you'd trained
but which slipped back to its wildness, the thing ran off.

For weeks you've tried luring it back with meat, milk,
a blue dish, a half pear. Every day the air

around the offering untrifled. You decide to sit outside for hours
for days, so still, so it might confuse you with tree or house, sniff

out its old stomping grounds, piss and look around. What you get
is cold and stiff, the question of how long you can wait filling

the hours you wait. The trees are just stoic, so fucking standby.
They know they know and won't show it.

Your dreams fill with rubber bands snapping in and out of shapes,
even in sleep your only desire: to see it stretch out

to rise and begin the journey back to what calls it.

The Persian poets

I love the Persian poets who wrote of chasing love,
of riding through the desert, looking for their beloved,

only to find at dawn the remnants of her campsite,
the pit from last night's fire, smoldering to the touch.

Always the lady has packed up and moved out
for another day of staying just-ahead.

The men sit next to ashes, writing calligraphy,
her name across the sand.

They imagine her here only hours before,
eyes heavy in the smoke, smothering the fire.

Those men, let's face it, they were writing for themselves.
They were telling stories of the greatness of their love

more than catching up to her. Those men,
maybe they found someone once they stopped traveling.

Settled down and made a home and occasionally
dreamed of the desert, the girl they never caught.

Meanwhile, she's out there, building fires.
Around her, sand dunes that used to teem with riders.

All these years ahead, she been riding past their love
and into absence, which was hers alone to fill.

Viva Glam!

A tree down the street is migrating
from gold to red, showy as a drag queen.
It shouts, "Viva Glam!"
    to each ogling passerby,
the neat lawns and already raked proceeds
standing in
for the whistles and claps of this nightclub act.
Is it wrong to love what is already loved?
Aren't there other and less dramatic pleasures?
      Oh, go light a match
and watch it burn to snuff, I say to that small voice,
the one that wants me to write about others, honest gestures,
and not the night I rimmed my eyes kohl black
and then sat down to cry
    so I could look up
and see my own face in the mirror,
smeared, gory.
    I've only got so much to give
and like a slide trombone
      it isn't subtle
but what is? Stars,
  enough with your coquetries.
Orion, pull back your arrow already
and shoot.

The blue hood

The shore

Before God made the shore
he divined a woman walking there,
her sorrow a deep hurt she could not name.

In response, he brought down water
and cupped it into an ocean for her.
He strewed waves with small things—
lavish strands of seaweed, fish like a bag of beads.
He made the whale breathe air so that on occasion
a giant would rise and be seen heaving.

Last, he placed in her heart knowledge
that he saw her sadness but did not take it;
he left it and left in place of its erasure
this company.

creation song

past memory
of the beginning
is the first
who played the reed

plucked one
for some other purpose
it was probably an accident
that he breathed out

his breath becoming
a long tube: tube long
becoming breath

his and out breathed he
that accident and probably
was it purpose, othersome,
for one plucked

the reed
who played first
the beginning
of memory passed

God speaks to Adam

Building you from earth
was like tightly packing a canoe
slipping in only
what I thought you'd need—
nothing extra—
for you were magnificent
but still a little boat
and I knew
the rowing would be hard.

Abandoned Mine
Chavies, Kentucky

Tucked at the end of a road we have trouble finding
a mine walled off sloppily with piles of stone.
Every year in the belly of summer
there's at least this place to retreat to,
a breeze wicking up from somewhere deep,
not as hot as the center of the earth at all.

Every few years or so, there's also the story of a child
stumbling in, adventuring in this shaft
or one of the dozens like it throughout the county.
Often, he comes out. Just as often, it feels,
he doesn't. Sometimes the tunnel's
too collapsed or there's danger of gas.

It's then they leave him,
reminder of the kind of soil
we're standing on, and all winter
spent dreaming, trying to see his body
in a pile of bodies waiting
under there, the secret store of hearts,
their dull maroon like gemstones
about to be born.

The first birth

was supposed to be a punishment, and certainly
some days the gestation felt that way: Eve's complaints

of pinching along her pelvic bone, the sleeplessness,
her feet swollen as gourds.

And they didn't know how long she would endure
this or if she would die by the end of it.

Despite their fears, Adam felt he would miss
her pregnancy when it was over, the engorged body,

its loveliness in water, those parts of her
that refused to sink,

as well as the ease with which he could read
her signs now—preoccupied as she was with fatigue and hunger,

basic needs
he could answer.

Whenever he found himself contemplating her eventual return
to the woman she was, the curious one who brought them here

by turning from him to prowl too deeply
into the garden, he grew anxious.

If she would not die in birth, then wasn't it only
a matter of time before he would find her crying,

her cheek against some cave wall as if listening
for the earth's store of voices, for comforts

other than his

After the change

Eve looked out among the herds of earth,
and saw the first real separation
for males and females,

her eyes lingering with marvel and grief
on the ewes, the cows and doe,
to think they went to sleep one night

and woke to ovaries like knots,
cupping wombs, intricacies and emptiness
in what used to be simple lives of sleeping and feeding.

That she took them with her when she changed,
that her alteration demanded the same
of the rest of the world was not meant to occur to her

in her moment of choice, though it stayed behind,
became the sure partner, the thing she never doubted after.
Even as she helped foal and felt the joy

of the new colt stumbling free—like the whispered consultation
as she kissed the swirled crowns of her children's heads
that it wasn't all bad—she still wished to cover

the mother's eyes in the exhausted sleep
of the afterbirth, to wish her back, to wish them all back
to that time before interiors.

Cain

In some stories, he's the firstborn.
In some stories, he's second.
In some stories, he and Abel each have twin sisters.
In others, they are the twins.
In all the stories, Cain is the one who kills Abel.
Slays is most often the verb.
Abel is the first on earth to be murdered.
His crime is being favored.
Cain is the first to murder, but not the first to break rules.
For that, we need only look to his parents.
In all stories, humans are on the earth for so little time
before they start hurting each other.

★

Sometimes now, those of us who've lost the ones we love
wake up with hearts pounding as if a voice has boomed in the room:
Where? "Where?" the air asks for the shape of the body.
And it's easy to see Cain as scofflaw trying to lie his way
out of this one, when God asks in a voice that seems to come
from within Cain and without, "Where is your brother?"
but it's also hard not to feel something for Cain in the aftermath
of the slaying: *Where? Where?*

★

What did Cain know of killing?
Before this he was a farmer,

spending his days in the fields,
sowing, rubbing grains between fingers.

Wherever they blew,
they landed to begin.

What to think of

Think of the spider you sealed in your grandmother's sun tea jar.
Think of it still there and breathing. Think of all the water in the world
and how it's true there's a limit, but tell that to the sailor stuck
amidst it without sight of land. That was the spider, sipping on air
like a child with a straw at the edge of a pond: this could go on

and did. It took weeks for that spider to give in, to die.
Every day you'd shake the jar to see its feet respond,
try to gain traction, until it was too predictable to do every day
and became once a week checking in, and then, the end of summer,
time to go home, time to think about feeding the beast or letting it go
or leaving it for your grandmother to find next time she was cleaning.

Think of the spider as if it's alive because that's how you last saw it.
Think of your experiment: to watch something die, to cause it.
Dividing the air into ever-smaller quotients is that moment. It seeks you now
as you once sought it: with power, with patience, with the ultimate say.

Passover

Imagine the dead whose deaths coincided
with this terrible, bloody night.
Imagine their shock to feel around them such newness
tinging the air, the glut of dead youth like an orchard
that has come to plague instead of fruit.

All those boys to be boys no more.
Egyptian or not. Overlord or not. Could you be a mother
and not think of them wistfully, the first time
their curls were brushed so that they shone.
Could you be a believer and not feel
how cruel and exact your god was.

The back way

There are moose and deer up here, so there's times driving the back way when
we near red splashes on the asphalt as if someone has spilled a bucket of paint,
a maroon that vibrates with iron. "It's blood," a kid says from my backseat, his
mom a vet so he would know, and I guess I should have, but for a long time,
I didn't. It was always strange painting acts—buckets falling off the backs
of trucks—I went to, and not the idea of what body—the size and damage
required to make the stain that big. Easier to think of all those pickups, careless
with their loads, gallons overturning. Sometimes a great big drum of the stuff.
That vat was for a church in a woods, its red walls thrumming in the night
when the lights are on and you can see the red glow from wherever you are
driving on this road.

Christmas Eve

It was a night like this—stinging clarity, the whole air
full of one metallic note, like a child chiming
on his triangle—that the shepherds were led to a stable.

The shepherds were cold and seeking.
A star was also on the lookout, ready to mark
where a baby had been born, though it found no milestones

to help it navigate, save other celestial organs
(for us, like looking into a crowd and expecting faces
to point north).

Somehow the star threaded the arms of constellations,
a game of red rover, and broke through, no star
before having moved from its orbit

except of course to fall.
For years, it levitated as if riding a carpet above
wherever the child might be playing. *It was hard*

to find you, the star wanted to say each time
it saw the boy racing after a toy or nestling into sleep
in some shaft of moonlight.

I looked into the spinning world.
I roamed from home to home and turned my back
on heaven to abide by you.

The boy went on sleeping or perhaps
occasionally looked up but looked past
the star to the dark spaces behind it,

to a future where the boy would no longer
be a boy and would become marked
in a different way.

With apologies to Hendrik Hertzberg, I will never finish reading your article

Nothing's worth doing if you can't do it compulsively is my latest motto:
that's why I knit to all hours, socks and long, wrenching scarves appearing
with the regularity of loyal visitors at a loved one's grave. The walls of my
house are painted, repainted like a slow eye blinking but there's this one
article, a few columns really, by Hertzberg that I just can't finish. I start
it three times a day, the subject never changing: the horizon of war, how it
cuts across all things. I want to read on; instead I keep flipping pages looking
for something that's easier. I don't want to be that kind of reader but I don't
want to see the way this must end either.

And for some reason, I keep thinking about the Amsterdam zoo, one of the
oldest in Europe. By the time I made it there, all the animals had gone crazy: the
elephant ramming his head into a steel door, his tusk jostled loose in its socket;
the sloth bear rocking back and forth, playing pendulum to an invisible clock;
armadillos in their red-lit nocturnal exhibit, taking turns trying to run up the
glass like track stars executing a drill.

But worst of all was the white wolf, the long trench he'd dug
just by pacing along his fence. The trench was thigh-deep
and wider than he. The wolf wouldn't slow or turn
no matter how much I called.

Emblem of grief, mobile and weary,
despite his beauty, his beautiful, beautiful
white fur, the long-snouted gaze.

The word *majestic* should have occurred
but couldn't because of the death on him,
that he'd run himself so thin

because of the desperation,
the back and forth,
the heart at the heart of this story
which is nothing but caged.

3 AM magician

is here again, ready to practice
our old trick: cutting me into bits.

He flourishes his velvet and taffeta cape,
the tatty edges tickling my cheek

as he prepares to insert the first blade.
It's always easy to give up the feet

to say good-bye to the inflexible
but consistent lower third,

trickier smiling through the stab
beneath my ribs.

Always these tears, the magician sighs,
not at all surprised. It's a moment of real

camaraderie. We both want this trick to work,
for me to grin a showstopping grin

so the invisible audience can applaud
and the houselights can be thrust back on.

He leans close, smells of talc,
sweat, an old choir robe.

One of these days, he downright purrs,
I will refuse to put you together right.

Instead of legs, I'll add on more arms,
another set of hands

to catch your sorrow
when it falls through.

The blue hood

Since I was born, I've been praying to something blue
and hooded inside me, straight from the cave

where early people gathered praying too
toward something they couldn't name.

It was invisible and mine, sure and mysterious
as an internal organ.

Once when we walked past a church with a Virgin statue out front,
my son said, "That is you," as if he too had seen the hood.

But that was before. For the first time, I've searched
and can't find the thrum, the ancient curve and the comfort

it carried inside me my whole life like a sail.

Some of those people who once gathered
must have left before.

Wandered through hills on their own.
The staggering vulnerability of the flat plains.

There must be such thing as coming back,
I tell myself, seeing only the soot-marked cave,

the emptiness that was always inside of what it held.

The swallowed world

Around me, a sea opens
until there is no land, until all time
washes back to Noah at sail

and he never lands, never launches
a dove to fly the tenuous flag
of an olive leaf in its beak.

It's as if there is no peace
between God and those he chose to spare
so the ark keeps floating until they die—

first the animals, then the people.
The creaking hull sailing on.

Sometime later, years, maybe decades—
does it matter with no one there to count?—
the wood gives out or the waves lap too hard,

taking the hulk down finally
to join the rest of the swallowed world.

Asylum

The afterlife, a big 1890s beach hotel,
initially as inviting as an asylum
with all those rooms and stark whites.
Once inside, you wonder: what was it
you thought you needed more
than these four good walls, the sunlight
tugging at the shade?

Your window looks out on empty sand
and hints at the god who runs this place,
everything here made in that image, liminal:
the shore asking where it ends;
the ocean answering, answers again,
equivocates.

The air gets confused:
is it related to or a part of water?
It bears the smallest aspergillum
into your room and sprinkles
the sheets so they are damp
when you lie down to sleep.

It is in your bed you think of holdings:
did you bring bags?

Are you the kind of person
who so easily lets go
or the kind who has a story to go with every dress,

every book and loose foreign coin?
You don't remember.
You could get up to check
but you stay in bed and let
the suitcase flicker into
and out of existence.

You are both kinds of people;
you are neither.

You were awake
and then you were asleep.

The little house

Squirrels, toss your acorns. Let the seeds sprout
in gutters, in a few weeks a fledgling forest
topping the roofline.

Termites, munch the sweet pulp of old doors,
leaving your dust piles finer than sand along thresholds.

Ants, line up.

Mice in the wiring, give birth to your retinue
of young and do it again.

All the wild tentatively held at bay by houses
here along the Gulf, come in.

All the chaos that nudges the screens and leans
to run its fingers through the dust of living order,
come in. The one I love

doesn't live here anymore.

galaxy of orphans

villanelle from the New York Times article "Billions of Lonely Planets..."
by Dennis Overbye

Billions of planets ejected are going their own lonely ways
distantly bound to stars at least ten times as far away as us from our sun—
a surprise, now it seems planets outnumber the stars.

Bent light acts as a magnifying glass in a vast field of night;
astronomers look for blips, for brightness—
billions of planets ejected going their own lonely ways.

They see planets passing without trailing hosts,
gravitational pinballs, too far apart to know if they're close.
A surprise, now it seems planets outnumber the stars.

The implications profound: not intricate chains, not concentric hoops
but solitary balloons bobbing in cold. Even as astronomers ponder,
billions of planets ejected are going their own lonely ways.

Whether planets are floating free or on a long leash,
prospects for life are dim, so space is emptier as it fills in—
a surprise, now it seems the planets outnumber the stars.

As usual, loneliness is the hole around which everything spins;
and those bright spots? Counting them is already less like wishing.
Billions of planets ejected are going their own lonely ways.
A surprise, now it seems the planets outnumber the stars.

The ghosts

The patting started a few years ago. I'd stir in the middle of the night to taps down my shins or the feeling of my blankets adjusting, as if from above, a set of hands, smoothing. At first I thought it was my grandmother. She'd just died and I missed her and I thought of the way she always made beds, the swoosh of her forearm over coverlet, a finishing gesture that I can only explain as looking similar to how the sensation felt. She used to roam at night and was known to come into rooms and straighten beds with bodies in them, so it made sense she'd keep old habits. For some reason, though, I stopped thinking it was her. Maybe because it was too much like her and her death was part of a breaking away from the known for me. I became aware of my own desires, of perhaps trying to keep her here, so I assigned the work to my grandfather who'd died the year before. He was passive in life, prone to sitting slung out in Barcaloungers. He was a long pale man with legs that seemed to erupt right out of his rib cage. I thought maybe he'd spent too long reclined. Now that his body was permanently so, he was free to go walking and didn't want to stop, on a tour of his family whom he loved very much and cried over in life. When emotional, he was prone to flustered patting and it made sense it was him, down by my ankles letting me know he thought it would be all right, no matter how dark it had gotten and the grief I was carrying that seemed to bore into my bones. I felt stiff on waking and realized even my grandfather's behavior was a way to comfort myself, when it could be just as easily my own legs talking to me, wanting me to get up and go. There was a lot to walk away from. So I understood, but I stayed put, and the legs sometimes still wake me up tingling. It makes no sense and I miss the feeling of a loved one reaching out across time and space for just a little gesture. The incredibleness of that journey was enough some mornings to make me stand up and start my own.

Some paths,

like these headed to Machu Picchu, are carved from rock,
giant slab steps that slant into the mountain like pool tables
tipped so you can almost hear the rattle and thunk
of orbs inside. You hesitate here at the edge, feeling that the others
who came before walked out on their knees, would've
walked over this mountain and out to the sea if need be,
and still farther out. Some paths are made for the desperate
and shake from them all who are not.

Others are puzzled from slate, chips that fit each other
and lead the way to house or down to the lake.
Frequented paths, thought-out ways,
every stone a fragment fallen from one great sheet
shattered long ago. The pieces arrayed as if
everything has a place in this world and ours
is on the path.

Some are made in grass, a stretch of bent blades
trailing the hill like a serpent lying in sun—
the place where they walked to get to where
they needed to be, the place that will disappear behind them.
Lovers, no doubt, the way they trample without regard,
the way they slink from view and the way the view pockets them
for the moment, holds the route they stepped, maybe
hand in hand or one right after the other.

The last paths are the ones in neglect, the spot where
a trail should open. Maybe in aerial photographs

the frail line of the once-followed is still visible,
but here in the thick, each stretch between tree trunks
is equally open as closed. A way once so known
as to be added to a map can go as a house dilapidates
with no owner, as a carcass breaks down with nothing inside.
Whatever else, the path is the people upon it
and to lose one is to lose them all over again.

After-fire

The woods are black, and dripping from the branches
that which soused them; water sluicing sockets.

It's a wood in post-disaster, after-fire—damp soot
heavy as clay.

Years from now it won't be bad to stand here,
the air feeling downright airy, the way it filters in

unfettered; a breeze just a breeze and not
something to watch out for, the way it breaks.

There's a hill near where men and women could've pulled
their silver blankets over them had the fire turned and lurched.

There's a way we know to curl into sod—not dead
but fighting death—and let earth palm us

like a magic trick.
The hill is behind me.

I am in the woods listening to the dripping,
feeling myself both soaked to the bone and dry as one.

After things burn, they lose dimension—
shapes shear back, charred to a black that rubs.

Any sapling or grass-nesting bird that comes here once
green returns is a kind of shade, an image arriving over

the truth of the landscape in this moment.
Like sky reflected in the water, filmiest net

stretched above a lasting dark.

Denning

Once our dog got sick and curled
under the back porch where only brown leaves went
to escape the rake. He entered in there to die
and a tremor of quiet rose through the house,
drawing me to his hole. I almost went down
on my knees when I saw him,
recognizing this instinct, his bared teeth
warning me to stay out of his way.

I think of this now because there is in me
something of the dog's timbre,
the house's reflective silence.
I am at the bottom of a cornucopian tunnel
without a sense of where that tunnel is or why
I went down it to begin with.

I say cornucopian because the world still yields
such bounty, whipstitched from maple,
the tannin ghosting of leaves on pavement.
Everything and all people seem to want
to hold me closer, but I am not out
and walking between them. I am deep down
and denning, and nothing—not you, not the stars
and the clear nights of their setting—can compete
with the well, the scurry scamper pull-away feeling,

except the rest of the dog's story,
that after two days he emerged, rickety

and standing, a different dog
from having laid in a hole. A different dog, too,
for having crawled out alive.

Triolet

To my grief my father spoke: after a death, there's a rushing
when we see the one we loved as he was, without us there,
the work of the holy spirit clearing away what was crushing.

To my grief my father spoke: after a death there's a rushing,
the last anger or hurt blown on until it blows out, an untrussing—
that blindness in you healed by his real absence in air.

To my grief my father spoke: after death there's a rushing.
We see who he really was, without us there.

The prayer

To pray means to follow the old paths
of the town cemetery, saying out
the words I find there, the long string
of *husband, father, wife, mother, son,*
sister, child, infant, beloved.

The rows make a tender field
where grief is in bloom and my prayer
is born not from pain or loss, but praise:
to say to what is—however briefly—
this is what was.

Eve at 80

Occasionally someone still confronts me,
teary-eyed at the paradise I denied him,

and there was the woman whose daughter died
in childbirth. "You," was all she said, and pointed,

"you," a word like a hole I fell into.

But I have earned some gravity now,
simply by having lived after living to begin with.

Wives at the market and men of the temple
speak less behind their hands and call outright to me,

"Mother."

It's true that I am mother to them, that by failing God,
I opened the way for others to please him better.

The moral of my scandal is the same as the seed pod,
as Adam's rib: wholeness must be broken

to find itself again.

Smokestack, 6 AM

Industrial waste unfurls in the pale, lit-from-beneath
sky, the smokestack looking as it occasionally does
beautiful, gold-tinged, and then the cloud of steam itself,
the way it seems to pause to gather its weight
before diffusing like the giant torso of a genie
and the world becomes what's rubbed the lamp,

but what wish? To whisk contamination from the air,
to repair to the water all its missing fish—dozens of varieties
so rare we didn't know them before they were gone?
Freud says all dreams are unfulfilled desires.
And wishes? Beneath everything else, they are only
and always the ways we want to be fixed.

The road I'm traveling this morning might still be visible
hundreds of years from now, when I am gone,
when maybe even all people are gone. Then, the ruins
of the smokestack, its effluvium snuffed, buildings
like rinds... And this might be my wish: in that time
of wholeness, a cherishing from the world, still full,
for what's broken. More than that. Because it's so rare,
that beauty becomes what's heaped, once-built.
That we, fragments that we are, might be missed.

The first place

I love you from
the first place
the black soil
the deep loam
of where I was made.
Down in the beginning
of me is you
and that time
we didn't yet live.
I was first and later
you were.

You were that white bird

Avian

Sometimes it was my job to flush the blind,
chasing from the teeth of that long grass
Canada geese, swamp fowl, flutter of neck leading body.

What became the challenge later was equating
these dead birds with the broken pottery of decoys
littering the back acre.

Once I asked for a feather from the kill,
and my uncle gave me a pen. He told me,
"Write one instead."

In defense of the tooth fairy
for Beth

At least she has a job.
Unlike some other bits with wings we could mention,
those most likely to be found loitering
at the babbling brook, their nonsense peals
indistinguishable from the river's notes.

And of all the fairies, she's the one
people are scared of, her sheer competence a threat.
Nothing like the dithering godmother variety
fussing over wands and gowns,
shoes that won't last the night.

Reliable as the fact we all grow older,
she shows up, undetected,
finds the hold under those pillows.
She's glimmer, gossamer, and something else—
hands quick as the pickpocket's,
with the tomb raider's gift
for undetected exchange.

Perhaps she's a criminal on parole,
a thousand years' good behavior
to make up for something in her past,
the memory of which comes back
each time she enters the blue realm
of a sleeping child, tooth like a penance,
waiting to be claimed.

Halloween

A grizzly bear and a pterosaur meet up
in my backseat. They eye each other—
the usual sizing up, despite the hundreds

of thousands of years' difference in their reigns.
One has talons and a beak like a jackknife.
The other has heft and strength.

The grizzly is the first to acknowledge
their shared love of fish. "We could both eat salmon,"
he says as if inviting the dinosaur to a dinner party,

a rustic one, considering the cave locale,
the stench of long winters spent sleeping,
leftover breath condensed on the ceiling.

The backseat is a riverbank in the Pacific Northwest,
dark trees gathering, a place these two creatures
might equally claim if there were no time,

no rock cliff behind them betraying with its sediment
the steady, steady slump toward change.

Dinosaur eggs

Less glorious than a *T. rex*'s jaw, large as a raft,
with teeth packed in like first, second, and third chances

less preposterous than the few samples of mummified skin
or stegosaurus plates, absurd petals of the prehistoric spine

less exciting even than the hundreds of hadrosaur vertebrae
dropped in the Plains like tokens around a toll plaza

are the eggs, indistinguishable at first from rocks
but for the repetition, the look of them together

nestled in a Morse code message of dot-dot-dot.
Eggs like doors blown off houses during a storm

found forlornly later, resting against hillsides,
impressing the wet host sand of a riverbank,

in any case long divorced
from the worlds they open.

Sky

Hard to pinpoint its beginning. Cloud level?
The air just above where our fingers touch
when reaching? Conveyor of birds and wind,
at night we pretend the ceiling is related to it
as pocket square to parachute.

But outside, looking at stars is looking through it.
Not lid, not containing. What hangs over us is
nothing, really. Even ashes, when you toss them up,
don't stay there.

A snowstorm every week for a month

It's sky that's fallen at my feet. Is that why
there is so much of it and heaps and heaps
before I'm done? At some point, I stop shoveling
against the snow and shovel with it,
by which I mean I have to believe

I am not trying to get anywhere down beneath.
I am not trying to get closer to the ground,
but biding my time on earth
in a lateral way, just moving.

There's a lot I could be thinking of as I stoop
and fling, but I find I think of none of it,
here in the quiet, the blankness around me
like all the chalk ever erased from boards,
particles fragilely attached to the words they were.

willow tree in snow

Last night's dusting outlines
all the little branches of the trees
so that walking out through them
is a revelation of eyelashes
like so much blinking after
coming out of the cave.
I tell myself to look quickly
before it melts, this framing
of the world I live in without seeing.
Then the willow tree on the corner,
like a woman bent over and brushing
the underside of her hair, the gold
and nubile reeds of every
fairy tale on display: Rapunzel
laying her head on a sill
or Rumpelstiltskin's gilded straw.
It's because the leaves are gone
that the tree is important to me.
I've been thinking about leaving,
going away so I can come back
appreciated. No more mature, I know,
than the child's dream of dying and spying
on her own funeral, deliciousness
to see regret paint all the sad faces.
But there are things about regret
the child imagining a black progression
can't know. It's not just leaving
I'm thinking of, but the parts of me

shed for the sake of the whole
the way the willow drops those elliptical
tongues on the sidewalk each fall, ceding
the engines of leaves to survive another season.
Maybe that's what's going on with me;
honed down to better weather all the weather,
my new smallness is a kind of battening.
But it feels like loss today, walking
under the willow with lines so distinctly drawn
and the momentary ability to see what's gone.

Sad bus

Like a bloodhound who's caught scent,
he's off, loudmouth near me on the bus,
announcing, "I got a niece who lost
50 pounds and now the boys are after
her. Maybe if I lost 20, I'd find me a girl."

Technically, he's closer to 100 overweight,
but who wants to get technical
with a fat man on this sad morning bus?

No one responds. He keeps talking:
"I'm one of the best dancers in Dover,
but nobody knows 'cuz nobody asks."

We've run through a whole history
of passenger pigeons but loneliness
is without end.

I'd turn and offer him my full face
if I thought it would help.

That's a lie.

It would help but I don't do it.
I keep looking straight ahead
and wait for someone else to shut
him up or turn my silence down.

The best dancer in Dover, the worst.
What does it matter, dancer?
Nobody's dancing here.

Building kites with the ghost of Virginia Woolf

En plein air, the painter paints the sea.
Between ocean and sky, there is no line
but misty intermingling.

These elements, kissing cousins in the molecular sphere,
share traits. Built on oxygen, they fit the shape
of any container that holds them.

It's a resemblance I notice in odd moments: trying to wring
the last sip from an empty cup, raiding the tackle box
for a fishing line and swivels to finish a kite.

I used to envy the amphibian's ability to find sustenance
in both worlds. Now I hear its cries when the pond thaws
as *too much, too much, too much* to reconcile

a groan renewed continually as the frog divvies
wet from dry, spring from winter, and then the mating,
a whole other set of halves to balance.

I take my kite into a field and I let it run with line.
It climbs. Or is it sinking?
Sometimes it seems things should mean more than they do,

that the difference between a red coat on a woman walking
and the same red coat on a woman lost underwater
should be more than just a deepening of color.

Brood

For a few weeks, a blue jay boarded here
in the shagbark hickory, magnificent
even among the magnificent of its species,

large and wildly chevroned, blue and white and black.
It attacked any bird, any cat, bumbling human,
to protect its partner open-beaked and on the nest.

The male and female jay are hard to tell apart,
harder after the eggs have cracked, when for a time
both parents feed the hatchlings with the intensity

of medics performing CPR, hunting and shuttling back
with the rhythm of chest compressions. A part of me
rises up: why do I hate the jays?

They live so penitently for one another and then nothing—
that devotion to a hunger outside their own, erased.
The parents fly off when the fledglings do, slipping cleanly

from the clutch. If a parent jay were to meet its offspring
later in the wild, it might never know, might give chase
with that kind of dive-bomb anger I watched it train

on every other creature in protection of the ones it made.
The Koran says, everything is perishing but God's face.
I was thinking something else: that love would last;

my brood, my stab at permanence. I found the blue jays' nest
blown free—a fleeting center, empty thatch, a clump of hair
pulled from a brush, as dead as that.

Pilgrims on the road

after Beato's 19th-century photographs of pilgrims and priests

They are not afraid of knowing, though they are more used to not,
to a road that travels where they cannot see.

Still, they say, *still I'm on it*. Some carry rocks as they move,
letting the extra weight remind them of the burden

of their human forms. *It's just like this stone.*
One day I'm going to put it down.

All over the road is the carrying.
They can carry so few things that each

becomes a symbol. The bedroll is the comfort
of the Lord. Their sleeves riffle

with the spirits of their elders. This spoon
is the part of the mind that doubts, always digging.

There are no photographs
of them sleeping, though it is assumed they did,

in great numbers, like a flock of swans
on the hill, looking out of place in their slumber

on the earth, their bodies kinked as if
being wrung out by the dream.

New Year's Day

It's warm after a cold night, and fog
rises into the air like all the badness
of that old year leaving, makes
licking white peaks of the roofs in town,
covers the fields with steeples.

When I drive home, the air won't be the same;
the sense of fleeing upward will be gone,
so I drive through, one eye on the stream
of every sad thing farewelling.

I let my grief leave too, and what lies down after that
is like faith, a blank sheet, what this year will be.

Paperwhite in winter
for KCG

It looks like an onion for a long time, and you can imagine
thinly slicing the bulb, frying it in butter. You see
your hands in this sauté vision as the sturdy knuckles
of an older European man, imagining even the little
blue cap you'd wear, the blade of the pocketknife
you'd use for the cutting.

The bloom is inside a sleeve and for two days
the sheath is what you receive,
the knobbed surface, the tension of something
that will not stay sealed. Then one morning, white trumpets—
one two three four five six on a green, a marching band
with members unseen but natty in spats.

On the sill, in glass, its tendril roots jam and tangle.
The green stalks, the applause of white. Out-
of-season bloom, the bulb emits what should have been
its dreaming: scenes that make no sense though
you take them, taste them, lick your lips and blow.

The white car

So far, I remember only one of those five important dreams Jung says we all have. You were driving the white car we used to own on a snowy night and went off an exit ramp into a guardrail. A power line came down and killed you. I found the car and it was up to me to drag you out. So many dreams are light, but that moment dropped through me as hard and fast as an anchor in water. I woke with a cry, the weight still there, straining my arms.

I think about the dream a few times a year and what it might mean beyond the truth that I love you, that I'm scared to lose you. And now that the white car is gone, I've had to learn to see it as something other than premonition. Fear's there and grief hovering, but there's also the reality of your body in the dream; it was as if I actually held you in my arms, despite the walls between that world and this, the death still safely tucked in your living body now. These days, what I bring back from the dream is the weight, how you leave an imprint I know, even in my sleep.

You were that white bird
(MM+NT)

You were that white bird, the one that came to him
and which he knew to be his love despite the long
distances you'd traveled and the metamorphosis
from expected form as human woman into pigeon dam.

The moments between you as bird and him as man
fit into a barely parted beak; they were that slim,
but when you died, he stopped working, dreaming,
loving anything else. He once held you in his hands.

You've wished as a woman now that he might be
on the front porch one morning, the magnolia bloom
he carries as creamy pale as your feathers had been.
But it doesn't even have to be that big.

The real moral from your life as the white bird
and the love that sprang from barest concurrence
is this: All love is really crumbs
to be scattered and retrieved.

Sometime in April

mixed with soil
and wet pavement
the scent like nothing else:

spring's ascent
hand over hand
from the molten core

drawing heat
behind it like a wake
igniting wicks

trees quicken, rehearse
flames; life lives inside
of life again.

The white mare

is dramatically swaybacked, downright
notched. To see her is to feel your gaze drop
like fruit from a tree
to the ground that cradles it, the deep U
of her spine.

Gamely the white mare wears
the groove, a hollow spot
like a cupped hand
from years of saddling.

Her owners, embarrassed
or out of a need to protect,
hide her behind the roadside stables.

I always find a way to point her out to you
as we drive past as if to say here is the proof
that partnering will change us

as if to say lie down with me
and leave your mark.

The eggs

The kids haphazardly dye
muddling the colors
making patterns explosive and continental
as the beginning of the world

while parents hover anxious
to teach them the proper steps,
careful calculations that lead to
brighter hues, eggs so deep blue

they seem hatched from the evening sky,
but life is more like what the kids know,
even how they got here around this table,
a half-dozen collisions of gametes internally.

Sometime long ago, where at first
there was no life, a single cell,
then another emerged,
replicated, became generations.

The eggs surface from inky washes, one
by one, as matchless as their makers.

Substance

You were like that falconer's bird,
old and nicked, the white head
gone tatty. With one lame wing,
it couldn't get anywhere but
beat against its perch every time
it saw a small creature thread
the near field, instinct
a sun with no setting.

★

You were like Maria Callas,
your clear gift ravaged—
used too readily, too heartily.
Even when the voice
was tattered, she kept singing
notes like battle flags
raised, victory stained
with all its costs.

★

You were like the rock
time and wind broke
until all that was left
were smaller parts, grit.
Until only a grain held on,
and even then, no atom within

did not know itself to be
substance standing up
to what sands us back.

Dear chick, dear hen-speck

Dear chick, dear hen-speck
you hatched yesterday
and I popped you whole
into my mouth where I held you
until your new beak
found my teeth and tapped.

Later when you are full-feathered
with the others under the house
clucking birth stories,
you'll have two to tell.

In this same way
I must have two endings,
a death like anyone else's
but also a bird launching from me,
my goodness,
my strangeness riding
its small back.

Acknowledgments

Grateful acknowledgment is made to the editors of the books and periodicals in which these poems have appeared:

"willow tree in snow" and "A snowstorm every week for a month" appeared in *the Aurorean*; "A snowstorm…" was also a featured poem on the website.

"Archetypal Renderings of the Male/Female Relationship," "My matryoshkas," and "The white mare" originally appeared in *Hunger Mountain*.

"God speaks to Adam" and "What to think of" were originally published in *Mid-American Review*.

"Brood" was featured on the New Hampshire State Council on the Arts Poet Laureate's Poet Showcase website and appears in *Poet Showcase*, the 2015 Hobblebush Books anthology of that feature.

"The blue hood" appeared in *Painted Bride Quarterly*.